Spot the Differences

Eagle or Falcon?

by Jamie Rice

Bullfrog Books

Ideas for Parents and Teachers

Bullfrog Books let children practice reading informational text at the earliest reading levels. Repetition, familiar words, and photo labels support early readers.

Before Reading

- Discuss the cover photo. What does it tell them?

- Look at the picture glossary together. Read and discuss the words.

Read the Book

- "Walk" through the book and look at the photos. Let the child ask questions. Point out the photo labels.

- Read the book to the child, or have him or her read independently.

After Reading

- Prompt the child to think more. Ask: What did you know about eagles and falcons before reading this book? What more would you like to learn?

Bullfrog Books are published by Jump!
5357 Penn Avenue South
Minneapolis, MN 55419
www.jumplibrary.com

Library of Congress Cataloging-in-Publication Data

Names: Rice, Jamie, author.
Title: Eagle or falcon? / by Jamie Rice.
Description: Minneapolis, MN: Jump!, Inc., [2023]
Series: Spot the differences | Includes index.
Audience: Ages 5–8
Identifiers: LCCN 2022011679 (print)
LCCN 2022011680 (ebook)
ISBN 9798885241588 (hardcover)
ISBN 9798885241595 (paperback)
ISBN 9798885241601 (ebook)
Subjects: LCSH: Eagles—Juvenile literature.
Falcons—Juvenile literature.
Classification: LCC QL696.F32 R533 2023 (print)
LCC QL696.F32 (ebook) | DDC 598.9/42—dc23/eng/20220401
LC record available at https://lccn.loc.gov/2022011679
LC ebook record available at https://lccn.loc.gov/2022011680

Editor: Katie Chanez
Designer: Emma Bersie

Photo Credits: Chris Hill/Shutterstock, cover (top); Randy G. Lubischer/Shutterstock, cover (bottom); aDam Wildlife/Shutterstock, 1 (left); Sergii Myronenko/Dreamstime, 1 (right); Fercast/Shutterstock, 3, 8–9; My Generations Art/Shutterstock, 4; gursimratphotography/Shutterstock, 5; Ondrej Prosicky/Shutterstock, 6–7 (top), 23br; Ken Griffiths/Shutterstock, 6–7 (bottom), 18–19, 23bm; A. Viduetsky/Shutterstock, 10–11, 23tl; Ian Grainger/Alamy, 12–13, 23tr; ARTISTIC om/Shutterstock, 14–15; Anatoliy Lukich/Shutterstock, 16–17, 23tm; Sergey Uryadnikov/Shutterstock, 20, 23bl; Dennis Jacobsen/Shutterstock, 21, 24 (bottom); Paul Reeves Photography/Shutterstock, 22 (left); Agnieszka Bacal/Shutterstock, 22 (right); Locomotive74/Shutterstock, 24 (top).

Printed in the United States of America at Corporate Graphics in North Mankato, Minnesota.

Table of Contents

An eagle often has yellow eyes.

A falcon often has dark eyes.

Which is this?

How to Use This Book

In this book, you will see pictures of both eagles and falcons. Can you tell which one is in each picture?

Hint: You can find the answers if you flip the book upside down!

Birds that Hunt

This is an eagle.

This is a falcon.

5

Both birds have feathers in many colors.

They look alike.

But they have differences.

Can you spot them?

Let's see!

eye

An eagle often has yellow eyes.

A falcon often has dark eyes.

Which is this?

Answer: eagle

Watch it fly!

An eagle has a wide tail.

A falcon's tail is narrow.

Which is this?

Answer: falcon

tail

11

wing

An eagle's wings
are rounded.

A falcon's are
pointed.

Which is this?

Answer: falcon

Both hunt.

Eagles often hunt fish.

Falcons often hunt mice.

Which is this?

Answer: eagle

An eagle builds a nest in a tree.

A falcon finds shelter among rocks.

Which is this?

Answer: eagle

Both lay eggs.
An eagle's are white.
A falcon's have
brown spots.
Who laid these?

Answer: falcon

egg

See and Compare

rounded wings

wide body and chest

yellow eyes

large hooked beak

wide tail

sharp talons

Falcon

pointed wings

brown or black eyes

narrow tail

sharp talons

narrow body and chest

small hooked beak

Quick Facts

Eagles and falcons are birds of prey. This means they hunt. They fly, lay eggs, and raise chicks. They are similar, but they have differences. Take a look!

Eagles

- build large nests high in trees
- hunt fish, reptiles, and small mammals
- usually lay two or three eggs at a time
- wings up to eight feet (2.4 meters) across

Falcons

- find shelters high on cliffs or among rocks
- hunt small birds, fish, and rodents
- usually lay three or four eggs at a time
- wings up to four feet (1.2 meters) across

Picture Glossary

narrow
Measuring a short distance from side to side.

nest
A place built by birds to live in and take care of their young.

pointed
Having a sharp end.

rounded
Having a curved edge.

shelter
A place that offers protection from bad weather or danger.

wide
Measuring a long distance from side to side.

Index

To Learn More

Finding more information is as easy as 1, 2, 3.

❶ Go to www.factsurfer.com

❷ Enter "eagleorfalcon?" into the search box.

❸ Choose your book to see a list of websites.